Field Trips

# At the Museum

By Sophie Geister-Jones

level
2
little blue
readers

www.littlebluehousebooks.com

Little Blue House is distributed by North Star Editions:
sales@northstareditions.com | 888-417-0195

Produced for Little Blue House by Red Line Editorial.

Photographs ©: Mypurgatoryyears/iStockphoto, cover; SeanPavonePhoto/iStockphoto, 4; monkeybusinessimages/iStockphoto, 6–7, 13, 22–23; skilpad/iStockphoto, 9; florin1961/iStockphoto, 10; Kirkikis/iStockphoto, 14–15; Oat_Phawat/iStockphoto, 17; FatCamera/iStockphoto, 18, 24 (top left); romrodinka/iStockphoto, 21 (top); Alex Potemkin/iStockphoto, 21 (bottom); Piksel/iStockphoto, 24 (top right) LeventKonuk/iStockphoto, 24 (bottom left); PhilipCacka/iStockphoto, 24 (bottom right)

**Library of Congress Control Number: 2019908618**

**ISBN**
978-1-64619-031-7 (hardcover)
978-1-64619-070-6 (paperback)
978-1-64619-109-3 (ebook pdf)
978-1-64619-148-2 (hosted ebook)

Printed in the United States of America
Mankato, MN
012020

# About the Author

Sophie Geister-Jones likes reading, spending time with her family, and eating cheese. She lives in Minnesota.

# Table of Contents

# At the Museum

We go on a field trip to the museum.

At the museum, we will learn different things.

We meet a guide.

He knows a lot

and answers all of

our questions.

guide

The museum has many old things.

We look at old paintings that were made long ago.

# Different Rooms

The museum has

different rooms.

One room has

old airplanes.

One room teaches us about our planet. The guide shows us a big globe.

Another room teaches us about dinosaurs. Dinosaurs lived long ago.

The museum has many kinds of art.
We look at paintings and sculptures.

costume

# Museum Fun

The museum has games.

We dress up in costumes.

We wear hats from long ago.

We play with toys at the museum.
We use our hands to learn.

We learn about science too. We have lots of fun at the museum.

# Glossary

**costumes**

**globe**

**dinosaur**

**painting**

# Index